OTHER POETRY COLLECTIONS BY DAVID GIANNINI

Stem
Stories
Sunlight As A Little Foe
The Future Only Rattles When You Pick It Up (selection)
Three (with Bob Arnold and John Levy)
Twelve At The Mill
What Moves/Moves Through
When We Savor What Is Simply There
Within Forever
You Can See

COMMENTS ON
SOME OF DAVID GIANNINI'S BOOKS:

On *SPAN OF THREAD*

David Giannini's "Span of Thread," which is a polyphonic, serio-playful, deep-structured celebration of life-in-language and language-in-life. This book is further proof that Giannini is among those who are saving American poetry from itself.

—Joseph Hutchison,
Poet Laureate of Colorado

"Span of Thread" is masterful, sinking the needle of Giannini's genius deep into the wonder of all things.

—Leo Seligsohn,
former critic for *Newsday*.

On *FACES SOMEWHERE WILD*

David Giannini's Faces Somewhere Wild spans his 45 years living and laboring in the Berkshire hill-towns of Massachusetts. Like the farmer whose face resembles what's fixed and moves around him, he is an astute observer of other faces. The man-with-the-broom who walks the streets making sweeping gestures reminds the poet, We are becoming motes or star dust. This resonates with the cosmic pedigree of the fallen drunk by the roadside: I drink the ancient atoms from a cask. Old Jane sees her dead daughter is a whitetail doe. The poet tracks the faces he sees for traces of the original faces somewhere wild, the revelation of something you were before all else, /something you were before all this. Giannini is the poet-hunter, who identifies himself as prey, in search of what waits at the threshold of expression: It wants to grab you by the throat. You don't turn away; /instead, you unbutton your shirt. Even as he fleshes the world with words, the poet strips it back to a superordinate mystery of atoms in super positions/in two or more planes at once. Giannini makes no attempt to resolve the paradox. Our guide through the Berkshires renders the vessel of creation as both full and empty. Feeling emptiness wing into you with its terror! Then owl to the empty nest. No reason not to have wept. Faces Somewhere Wild is a perch where the burden of mortality touches our hearts. Highly recommended.

—Paul Pines

On *POROUS BORDERS*

In his latest collection, David Giannini works the "porous borders" between poetry and prose, tragedy and whimsy, gravity and absurdity, to offer up a grab bag of playful, thought-provoking pleasures that are "something more than real" but rather "meta-real, hyper-real, surreal, irreal," as befits a world in which "the real thing . . . is always at least partly a drafty, shifty, get-my-drift, daffy alembic grab-bag, wifty and makeshift." Not so these verbal gems, whose fancy and fantasy enriches their resonance in an alchemy akin to "light tr[ying] to shed from a dark place to golden itself" or those answers "behind every door . . . eavesdrop[ping] on the deft noise of questions" which we hadn't realized were troubling us, until encountering this unique and delightful book.　　—Susan Lewis,

editor of *Posit*, author of *Heisenberg's Salon*

In these vertical prose poems, Porous (more Stevens's Crispin than Berryman's Henry) takes us through condensed narratives to grand myth and philosophy. Correspondence here leads to contradiction: "each is a shutter of the other." And along the way devilish angels offer "another place, also of poetry, a place of lyric dissociation, a locus" on the page -- these "micro-mono-liths" swirl with macro-spin.　　— Dennis Barone

On *STEM*

These poems know a mysterious grace. They hover lightly about the imminent birth of things, taking shape from the clench-ing & declension of the story locked in the human form. The human they propose is a sum of the covert intelligence of the

world when it "works", an ear minutely attuned to the folding
* unfolding of creation. Flight, grace, transparency is how they
tread, bending neither the grass nor the flowers that *inch out
/ lean against gravity*. As Guillevic said, they do to light what
light does to them.   — Andrei Codrescu

David Giannini is one of the most interesting and original of
American poets.   —James Laughlin

On *RIM/WAVE*
This beautiful book is actually two books in one. Rim is the fic-
tional account of the title character, a farmhand who both lives
and works within the harshness of the physical world, and who
sees beyond it to the spiritual and the metaphysical. Whether
we call this a prose poem or a story told in the language of
poetry, this is a powerful narrative of a character I won't soon
forget. The story is further enhanced by representations of
woodcuts by Franklin Feldman. The second part of this impres-
sive work is a collection of poems called To the Wave, Poetry
at Seacoasts. In these poems Giannini reflects on people he has
loved, and on the earth, water, and air of and around the ocean
and the animals that inhabit that space. Many of these poems,
though short, resonate deeply, and few poets get so much from
so few words. These two books complement each other through
Giannini's great skill with language and his ability to join the
concrete and the abstract. It's poetry grounded in the earth.
                        —Mark Farrington,
       Program Director M.A. & Graduate Certificate in Teaching Writing,
                        The Johns Hopkins University

The
Future
Only
Rattles
When
You
Pick
It
Up

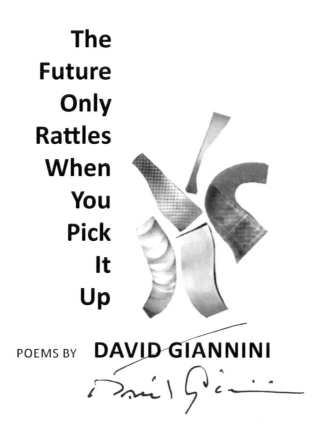

POEMS BY **DAVID GIANNINI**

DOS MADRES

2018

DOS MADRES PRESS INC.

P.O.Box 294, Loveland, Ohio 45140

www.dosmadres.com   editor@dosmadres.com

Dos Madres is dedicated to the belief that the small press is essential
to the vitality of contemporary literature as a carrier of the new voice,
as well as the older, sometimes forgotten voices of the past. And in an
ever more virtual world, to the creation of fine books pleasing to the
eye and hand.

Dos Madres is named in honor of Vera Murphy and Libbie Hughes,
the "Dos Madres" whose contributions have made this press possible.

Dos Madres Press, Inc. is an Ohio Not For Profit Corporation and a
501 (c) (3) qualified public charity. Contributions are tax deductible.

Executive Editor: Robert J. Murphy

Illustration & Book Design: Elizabeth H. Murphy
www.illusionstudios.net

Typeset in Adobe Garamond Pro

ISBN 978-1-939929-91-4

Library of Congress Control Number: 2017953083

First Edition

ACKNOWLEDGEMENTS

The author wishes to thank all editors, and one curator, for the following publications:

Birds, A Flight of Poems (anthology, New Feral Press,) "Bonelast."

Bongos, (Japan), "November: Thanksgiving Cornfield" was first published as "Thanksgiving Cornfield" in a different version online.

Caliban (online, issue #27) "A Moment Before Turning to Another Channel," and "Challenge."

Caliban (online, issue #29) "That Country"

Country Valley Press, "Vanishing;" "Vertical Bolt, An Assay;" "Continental Divide."

In the West of Ireland (anthology), the untitled poem beginning "What is uncommon."

Jacob's Pillow Dance Festival, "Figninto (A Blindness.)"

Lilliput Review, the last eight words of "Buona Notte" considered a haiku.

Longhouse, the first 11 lines of "That Country" were first published as a brief prosepoem, now lineated and expanded in this book.

Masspoetry.org, online 7/14, "Vertical Bolt, An Assay."

Merde Vol. I, No. 2, "Vertical Bolt, An Assay," "Response Sieve."

New Feral Press, "Returning Letter;" "Inverse Mirror."

Noon, A Magazine of the Short Poem (Japan), "A Moment Before Breakfast" appeared vertically lineated.

Oyster Boy Review, "Sharing 70% of the Human Genome;" "Inverse Mirror."

Stone Walls II, Issue 6, "Free Throw On the Way To the Airport. . . ."

"Figninto (A Blindness)" was a featured broadside exhibited at The Jacob's Pillow Dance Festival during their 75th anniversary in 2007—special thanks to Norton Owen, Director of Preservation at Jacob's Pillow.

"A Speaking Born of Us" (first poem in suite) was first published as a broadside from Cityful Press.

"Rickshaw Chasm, 12 Graphs" was published in a separate, limited edition from New Feral Press and illustrated with collages by John Digby.

For Pam, always

TABLE OF CONTENTS

I

II

III

Vertical Prosepoems

I

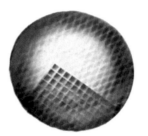

WORKERS

Who would condemn
small children? What
if, with Sisyphus,
toddlers were forced to roll

small stones beside him
on the long push uphill
before the terrible trek
back, all of them compelled

to repeat their acts forever?
Perhaps loneliness
would lessen for a while
and love increase; but could

any of us in this century
bear to look even at pebbles
without sensing those kids
forced to stone? Sisyphus kept

and keeps on. . . the children
grow jagged, sometimes
round. We look at their faces
in the rock of mountains,

and at times they are visible
inside geodes—tips of
noses sticking out, shiny,
purple from exposure.

FREE THROW ON THE WAY TO THE AIRPORT BEFORE RESISTANCE AFTER THE WOULD-BE DICTATOR TAKES OFFICE

With a ball less cold than rocks
on a freezing day, what drives a hooded boy
and girl shooting hoops by a lazy loop
of river, except being young in the air

and practice under clouds; until, over
time, what is baleful for each
sinks in, and rules tossed downriver
float or drop with the gallimaufry of it all.

I would like to call tears merely results
of an onion for them; but all of us now
weep at the world, with the world, offer
each other to each other. It is a kind

of sacrifice, kind in itself, as we pass
(as we are always passing) through security
to the other side—from bouncing on laps
and dribbling, to the unknown planes ahead.

THAT COUNTRY

They were warnable, the people of that country,
and not warned.
                             Their flesh
burns in the newscasts
coloring in the fact

of assault.

                High in the trees
every nest's empty. There's silence across wheat
of the full fields the elders
and the children
hacked.

                How it is that

wind rushes ahead of its own core, which is still

air; that there are human bodies fleeing

until they halt
and wait for the characters inside them

to catch up, the static ones
who would crackle and hiss
against betrayals;
                        that they will

move beyond trees
        over the rough roads
                into the cities

where the eyes of their countrymen turn

into burning stones.

WAVE THEORY AT THE AIRPORT

Throwing our hands up,
we wave wildly
until we think we've grabbed
your attention, although we no longer know
you. We gesture for you to come
through the cloud of strangers,
through shafts of light
making a golden cage, packing us together
until our separate darknesses
squeeze into one, and the cage-being
steps forward
glowing more and more fiercely,
a lion made of light
gripping us until we feel conveyed
within a brilliant package
yet to be claimed.

THE HEARING

Does anyone else hear that
                low pitch at night

deepening space before the sun, or care that such vox

may issue from neither clock-
                radio, bird, person,

nor star moving something out of its shivering mouth

of light? It seems to bounce /
                then teeter on frequencies

before death or its original inspiration, breath

pulls us like sorrow
                dragging that weight

which must be our own.

NOVEMBER /
THANKSGIVING CORNFIELD

Wind. Dry
    stalks—
I am

grateful for
    this
raw

music, for
    what is
missing, for

what has
    been
eaten

away, for
    these
slaps of

leaves, this
    old
family, most

still
    upright /
moving /

shaking to
    the same
rasp.

TERRARIUM

Inside this
glassed-in earth
a dragonfly

        hatched—wings
        knocking at
        the lock.

Faces
close
we sensed

        it
        trying to
        roam

beyond its
clear birth /
tomb.

        Outside, winter—
        a neighbor
        boy pressed

our windows
looking
through wings.

BEFORE WE KNOW

He did as chore what he did in mind
after that   First the unthought thing
caught in his body and its ways
lifting branches of snow   breaking
icicles along path   because all was body

and how it taught itself to move
face made by wind   to be refulgent
and auric   ice cleat boot tread
traction crampon   chain spikes
what it wore to cross

backyard glaze   to stacks of split
logs to serve to heat indoors   and return
the man within   to have in mind
what body had in deed done   not less for
another   more and more   for her.

CONSCIOUSNESS, A VALENTINE

At lake's edge, where sand seems to disappear, water
at my toes. We seem to know we are 75-78% water
at birth. Adult, I am closer to 60% water,
and you, as woman, to 55% water.

Yet I am also in here, as not 40% water,
aware and self-aware with more than water.
I sense you there and here of water
and something other than water.

With what do we love other than water?
Speak to the water :
what the other and water
believe of it is poetry. Through water

I love you with all of my other and water.

SHARING 70% OF THE HUMAN GENOME

The thug inside everyone's dreams
leans in from infinity, moving at the pace of an orchard,

then muscle cars speeding track.

Thug means   what teems   as real.

Take your pick. Raw fist
of roses, tire spin, apple, pretty little bashing clouds,

chaos a form of charisma.

It's always thug time in the old enigmas—
legerdemain / whack

of some fact, for instance humans: 14,000 genes in common
with the deep-sea acorn worm. Therefore save yourself

an ocean, another day in.

PETRARCH: SONNET 164

(erasure from a translation by A.Z. Foreman)

the hush of   sky,
                    holds   birds,
Night drives
          waveless,   only I
Still see   and rave
              of sweet pain
          and tears,
          thoughts of Her are all

Thus   sweet and bitter draughts
      from a   living fountain
                    both heal   and deal
          my   sea
          a thousand births and deaths a day
So far

11

DILEMMA

1.

To sense being as trees and as rain
then as air between the desire to be
rooted and the terrible falling /

         never knowing in that sinking
         of one to roots of another
         what inter-world may rise.

2.

Dear Atlas, Dear Freud,

The world is apocryphal and coy,
in mind held up mightily—oh, but

         what world
         is meant
         by that? Which

         world sifts
         us into what
         the World is?

3.

Once again, the stones mean to stay.

MAYSONG OTHER

I hoe black soil   plant seed and seedlings
then tamp stakes   sweat darkening

small rocks   until something   or other
dances in me   and I think   the invisible insists

its own parthenogenesis   this rock baby
wee crack mouth   twist-and-pout

as I raise it on out   and now tell me only if
it doesn't have the smile   of something *other*.

MAYSONG OTHER, 2:
SILLY WITH FATIGUE

Wearing a torn slub knit T-shirt
dun with soil,
      hee-haw, he
          hoed. He seeded
rows of beans and folded loopy channels shut
before thunder and a slosh of rain.

The garden, planted, he entered
fog in
      the mind of
          a nincompoop,
a force of a different clutter—horse
nickers, jester-hat-bee-balm, dog,

and with a knick-knack paddy whack
this old gent
      went howling
          tunes—lots
of rock and jazz disc music at home
kicking out the jams and the fog. He said:

Afoot and night-larded I take to the groping toe,
then collapse
      as an ash-heap
          spreading across
a continuum of colored pillows—
I'm in the spectrum, don't come in. Oh, my

dust needs a dream of waking seeds—
what lies
      just beyond
          sleep and what
I am, what event beyond vanishing,
what lies?

VANISHING

as parsley in
farm hands

                    as farm family drunk
                        deer hunters

as dear hapless
burly girlies

                         as pickups and
                            guys with

work-busted
guts some

                            fuckers and
                     meadow meows

bales a bull
cows a few

                          tending next
                     to the bearable

rightness of
spiky objects

                            lemonade
                             dust.

NOCTUARY

4 a.m.

Dark. I turn
lights on at home—
two robins

                              begin beating
                        their wings against
                                  windows,

beat themselves
to death before
I can switch lights off.

                        They may have been
                               traveling by
                  starlight and just arrived

back north for spring,
and mistook lamplight
for sunlight.

                           Later, you awake,
                              I find imprints
                      from feathers on glass.

Rust-
red and pale
orange breasts of

                      the pair on ground.
                          What departs
           still stands in the whole.

Even so,
the shame of loss
weighs us.

                           Many poets
                            now dead
                       beat themselves

against transparencies
and light. An artist
disappears in

                          order to make
                       something else
                             appear.

I wish
those
birds. . . .

BROOK. . .

with small bones
eddying. Do they want
out? To be
                (again)
articulate?

Raccoon tracks
in mud of the bank.
                        And scat
of what? What
                night-
creature eyed stars in water?

May our bones spin bright,
flow and be
nabbed configurants of a vast
joint
        like the Crab

N   E   B   U   L   A

CONTINENTAL DIVIDE

To Andrew Schelling

Night is an infant with her eyes shut,

     and because we made her
we are behind her
           pupils in the ovaldark.

*

Asleep or not, she is, already, steadfastly herself, a certain
stubbornness her event, She-Who-Is-Like-The-Rocks.

*

Each morning, she opens
and brings us out to the ledge of her awakening
west of the Divide—steep jagged cliffs, pinnacles,
spires, fragile abutments, angles
and blocks of granite
   as though a child had
haphazardly
   stacked
them.

*

The honorable way to name a thing is to first see what path it's on, apply the name befitting the way of it, watch thing-with-name become indistinguishable from what it moves upon and through.

*

      This is the way of it, ever:

Because we made her
She-Who-Is-Like-The-Rocks
             when stone chips
off
    and hits
            the canyon floor

talk obtains in her silence

      and coyote runs a long way off.

"FIGNINTO (A BLINDNESS)"

Based on a dance performed by *Salia ni Seydou*,
a West African dance company, at Jacob's Pillow Dance Festival
during its 75th anniversary season in 2007.

With hands only

building the only road

      out from

   the African

dunes. . .

      to dance

    blind grains a man's

sun hollow

      gourd of

   light's

sand poured

      to bake

to bury

   to become

    duned: still life

     from which no hands escape.

THANKS FOR WHAT DOES
AND DOESN'T EXIST

Moonlight causes the statue of a woman
to open her eyes.

It is as late as it is early.

Thicket of hours
until first light strikes her

and every wide-eyed animal

inhabits the same perceptions
of bronze: still, silent, no living scent.

Sunlight causes the statue of a woman

to open her mouth. As she did
after crossing herself before

fire and smoke lay down their arms,

her mother sifting ashes
and bashed bone, wailing,

imploring even the moon

to remember the charred tooth
of Joan of Arc

still

displayed.

BONELAST

Blue heron, even as you tilt

    over the reflecting lake

        you can never know

your face won't last

    as long as your skull. So it is

        with a sad, full

understanding that

    we admire this:

        your unknowing.

FIELD NOTES / PAINTER'S EYE

red

1.

A lipsticked girl on the path—
mouth red
           against pale skin,
going with her mother
                for a swim.

2.

A blip in the swell-bent
blackberry canes—
                only the flick
of its tail in thicket,
             male
cardinal
      full on.

3.

Not to let land-and-lake be decoy
for this essence I want to hold
as shape, size, scale, and process:

                        red

as that painted dot
found in the Neanderthals' cave
in Gibraltar, or as Miro's

                      The Red Spot,

as event

           beyond its occurrence
in the living frames
of bird and child   (mother standing by.)

THEY

glacial boulder, Florida Mountain, Massachusetts

They were not there They were here when They said.
They kept saying. They kept saying
that the boulder was really there,
if I walked. If I walked
through dense woods—I did.

When I found the location that They had described, I found
what appeared: a single, immense boulder, high as a herd of
elephants standing in a tight circle, heads in, rumps out, and
somehow resolved into the being of stone.

They were not there or here when They said.
What They had said appeared and appeared to be
true. It appeared, so I approached the stone,
the elephantine one. Very slim, pointed birches stood around,
like white spears.

The more I looked at the boulder, walked its circumference, the
thicker the air became between us. I walked closer, as They had
suggested. The air grew more dense, more occlusive. They had
not suggested this, They said.

The closer I walked toward the boulder the greater
the distance between us. How can this be, I thought,
that what is closer is also farther away? I walked
closer. It was farther. It was
also further.

It now seemed that there were miles between us. Or feet. What did They say that They had not said? There were millennia between us. What did They? There was great distance somehow intimate. It now seemed that They.

There were elephants or what appeared to be
elephants, far yet very close, very close, but far,
and as I looked they became covered. They became
covered with hair, with thick hair. Ice-age hair.
They were that near and far.

What They had said They say. I said what They said. Then I felt myself covered with fur. My body began to stink. What in a man could and can walk up and down the helix of his own being? It is further than we think and so here.

The sun began to set. The elephants, the stone,
became another thing, soon gone—images at rest
tend to death; images in motion tend to remains. In
darkness They say what They had said. I said and say
what They had said and say.

We all hear because we heard. Sudden scream of something nasty in the woods—went away. Then what it was came back, came closer, as it always did and does, They say. It all seemed what we heard. It all preferred to seem.

They were not there They were here when They said.
They were here and there when They said.
Keep fire. Go on. Go on
for as long as forever is, for as long
as it is, or was, They said.

INVERSE MIRROR

A man fiercely tight in himself, stone-like,
nevertheless scrabbled forward along a massif

and felt a fierce break in the clouds
where a woman fiercely light, cloud-like, floated

over the man fiercely tight in himself, stone-
like, and so on they went into the master task

of reflections, where one was not the other
and the other was not the one, and both upon

reflection found themselves curiously inverse,
one up, one down, each wanting to speak,

wanting truth, but knowing that the last word
is never in, though it is waiting.

II

A Speaking Born of Us

A SPEAKING BORN OF US

Tell all the truth but tell it slant —Emily Dickinson

suite: 10 poems for Pam

1.

What begins
is this
  Companionship
inhabited more
deeply
  Depth
of your secret
eyes mine our pupils
wide with each other
naturally
   Not *will*
(never a matter
of that)
   Desire
to open
desire further more
than touch
tells
  An intelligence
of bone skin light
of the boundaries
between us
   and a speaking
quietly
   with such force
of hunger.

2.

Edge of the lake   desire's
edge   water taking me   takes
my thighs   my breasts   out to
depths   thrusts of watersprings
around and into   now the lake comes
quiet   as my eyes   as my breaths
woman-in-man   man-in-woman   heart of
heart knowing the unity of this
desire remaining desire

Now the shore   speaks   where water
meets land   laps at land   the two
saying what is   what is inevitable
in the body   is body-time   force of
the field it is   always becoming
as we   become   with our flesh come
to that further range   range of
the source   yet intimate   known
intimate course   known these years

3.

What is uncommon   if natural
to a woman   becomes her

sorrow-mixed-with-fight

'the fighting Irish'
and escaped Jew
within her

singular and epic

system like a sphere
Curving, because thus curves

the tear. . .

stronger than the tug's
yank
that brought her
forebears in
        to harbor. . . .

4.

After all
day listening hard
to those who cry
alone　　alone
deploring that they are. . .

you drive

home—every
female purple
finch at
　　　　the feeder
hovers
　　　　whereas the males
land hard
　　　　and grab—
no one is more
　　　　　　or less
hungry—the world's

seeded the people sad.

36

5.

We were speaking of the invisible
leaves at night
          under opossum feet

speaking in sunlight of that
shifting and routing that goes on
                    as we do at times

feeling we have made
identifications beyond
            the muddle

other times knowing
we have lost the thing at hand
                having gained

too much ground with that
realness we were looking for
                and how

even it sometimes seems
abstract
      beyond our means

as if not we
but it
      plays 'possum.

6.

Anger is also what is around it—

smolder border
then
the burning
foliage into
whims on the mend

Wind
        berates

deliberate   distance

            liberates
                        stance

as
between trees
we clarify
the ruthlessness
received.

7.

Many times   or most   we are
present to each other   the way
our talk is   the way our talking is
a form   a form of being   of being
present   of feeling our talk inlaid
inlaid with silence   silence as
an invisible jewel   in a setting
of syntax   a setting of sound
many times   or most   the tone is true
bright within the talk and silence we hold

Many times   or most   the spaces
between our words   placing in talk
are not gaps   they are infusions
of our presences   inlaid   but motioning
in motion   but fused   each with each
mounting   set   but mounting until a third
is made   of our silences and sounds
a third presence made   as light intoned somehow
most times   a form of love   of being true
third being formed from tones of talk we fuse.

8.

To start with
a feather
            in the air,
no wind. . .
                a pebble
for no reason
rolling from a larger stone. . .
petals
            into sun. . .

and what with one thing
and another, nightfall
and a star,

where are we, Pam,
where we are?

In the poetry of moments
the course of being

mere,

merely ourselves.

9.

Saddles & dark eyes

the creak in quiet
of a field
                fat with
fireflies—
                life
lit with live

stars—& horses
striving in us

wild   wild thighs.

10.

I'm awake it seems to hear the rain
at the window beyond your sleep

to meet your hair with my hand in the dark
feel it misted then in stir

further and further fur on the pillow
a panther metaphysics of address

space the roar you'll wake to
black animal around blue sky.

III

Vertical Prosepoems

His special gift is to bring these two processes, inquiry and narration, into a conjunction, making things up as he discovers them and discovering them as he makes them up. He never works to a plan, and so his prose stays close to the thought processes of a writer working out what to say next and responding to what he has, perhaps mistakenly, just said.

— *NY Times* on novelist, Javier Marias

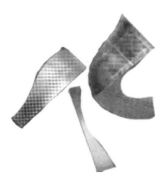

VERTICAL BOLT, An Assay

Prosepoetry (as I spell it) is a sort of Dutch door on a cabin in the woods. The larger, heavier, lower half is prose; the upper shorter half is poetry. One key unlocks both, while a vertical bolt unlocks the poetry that then can swing on its own hinge. One may look in or out upon things, but the same things viewed from the top door take on different significance since the bottom half, if remaining shut, may serve to protect. For instance, one may vocally chase a bear from the upper door while feeling protected by

the lower one; or one may invite a dog or an owl to come closer and, if friendly, the dog may come through the door of prose, an entry-point no self-serving owl would ever enter. Owl enters through the top. It enters through the opening of poetry, silently at first, then what a hoot! There may be more owls in poetry, therefore. One makes an attempt to invite dog and owl at the same time, train them until they desire to go together, not exactly like lovers, but steady. It seems an impossible relationship, but it really is one on the path to the resolution of paradox, and it has a certain scruffy plausibility in training. Neither dog nor owl will speak of marriage, only sex and syntax. The wag occasionally ruffles feathers. The beak is mightier than the muzzle, and more precise. They are contained in a rectangle, a page, but their true shapes, when viewed together, live inside it as one from which the shadow of an angel is sometimes cast. To view is to listen. Listening is also a door.

RETURNING GIFT

for M.L.

An old lover has kindly mailed me the antique hand-mirror I gave her, handle and body of silvered tin with cherubim pressed in relief. I haven't seen her or the mirror in 25 years!

The mirror always contained unseen broken bits between the glass and those tinsome heavenly bodies, maybe shards of backing that rattled when the mirror was lifted, as if the result of the hands that held it up to the faces that peered with their own backings.

And there were always clouds in the glass—unreflected nimbus and cumulus—present in the circle, so that anyone looking into the mirror would see their face in a kind of sky, sometimes with an eyeball, half a brow, partial lips, a cheek in rainy weather, a nose with a shadow, and so forth—no one could see themselves clearly or whole.

That sky is cloudier now. As I shake it, raspy knocks issue from the glass of old desires while the unseen comes more and more to occlude. Will the glass cloud over completely, its night hold no stars?

The future only rattles when you pick it up.

AFTER SHE DIED, I MOVED ONTO ANOTHER

...color, though it enabled the flooded look, like that of an engulfing weather front. . . . ."
    —Peter Schjeldahl in "The New Yorker", 9.22.2014

Her face had a flooded look, like that of an engulfing weather front, so that she appeared to keep many emotions, with their possibilities of storm and wind, for long periods before deciding what to purvey, which way to blow or otherwise assail someone she had lured to the island, until she could return pacifically to a beach. I still think of her sometimes as shapely and pointed as a conch shell somehow crossed with a porcelain doll. Shell-doll.

She was an edge-parker of expressions, ones too fleeting for others to grasp, until it was far too late for them, and they died by eating out of her own, barometric hand, the one that could feel so pleasantly dry and warm to the touch, at first, until its pressure dropped. I should know, because I am the only one, so far as I can tell, to have survived her attempt to grip, because I am composed entirely of shadow, no substance, and because I cast wherever I move.

I frequently accompanied her and often slipped onto her shoes and covered the drops of blood there as she stood and admired her murderous work. In effect, I was her accomplice, a fate formerly relieved only when she was in a sunny mood and only at noon.

MINA & PLATO

One of our cats, Mina, spots a gecko on window blinds she can't get at. When the gecko hides on the other side of a slat, the cat is as blind to it as it is to the cat. It is a game of blind-and-seek, of what is sensed to be there, though unseen, so the cat listens for the least stir and sniffs for scent, for what is real to her. She doesn't yet realize that I have caught the creature gently and already released it outside. What is real for me is outside while what is real for the cat remains on the other side of a blind. It could just as easily have turned out that the cat caught the gecko at some point I didn't know and so I still believed that the creature was there, elusive, holding on, and that I was blind-sided by that, by such belief in what I thought was real. My belief and belief itself is a kind of galaxy, and as everyone knows: if you come to the galaxy inside a truth, the unconjured ones will come, dressed in prodigious natural illusions like the colors of certain lizards, chameleons or their relative geckos. Will you be ready to receive them? Here kitty, here kitty kitty. . . .

ALTERNATE TENDENCY

I was about to eat my sea-side breakfast and was just-lifting my first spoonful when a man slipped on the patio floor and tore his Achilles tendon on the iron rung of a chair next to me, so painful. I helped him into the ambulance, poor fellow. When he returned from the hospital, big soft blue boot on his foot, I told him that I could now think of him swimming in the ocean with his blue booty a sort of miniature foot-shaped sea floating with him, a sea on the Sea. "That makes little sense," he said, "but on the other hand no shape is the "real shape" of the sea, and as feet keep falling into the wrong rungs, boots keep falling into the wrong sea," he added, making even less sense, "but at least now I can think of myself as having a certain tendon sea." Then he told me, "With everything crude we have free passage to refine what we think, as if thinking proves things can reduce ideally, until they are as many sea horses or, for that matter, iron filings, in our minds; and even though we try to tattle on the ultimate magnet or sea, to find some larger truth, alas, we are merely slammed by and into a greater force, maybe part sea, part iron, even part horse." Ahem, what has any of this really to do with the fact that I missed breakfast and you've torn your tendon? I asked. Who are you, anyway, and what are you doing on my patio, at my table? "Pass the cornflakes," he said, as he lifted his blue sea to the chair beside him, grains of sand spilling like so many filings onto its iron seat stamped with seahorses.

MR. APOPHASIS

When he woke, he noticed the index finger on the sheet beside him. The finger was pointing at him, but occasionally flexed and shifted direction as if pointing to an ear. The difficulty, thought the man, lies in not knowing if I am being accused of something or merely pointed at as one indicates a direction for the location to which one must travel; or else the finger pointing surely toward an ear means that I must articulate clearly. There are balances between the two, the man thought, as he lay there, head upon his pillow, and I wouldn't want to mention, having had this stroke, feeling that I am nothing more than an accused location unable to speak.

SOAP & WATER

We all try to clean ourselves, but doing so actually disturbs the invisible, said the nurse. So many micro-colonies of fauna and flora are spread from you to your shower which becomes a bacterial arena. So surgeons don't shower before they operate. At least, they're wise not to, wise for the sake of you, the patient. A patient shouldn't shower beforehand, either. Notice that I haven't offered you a bath before your brain operation. All the old skin of your skull protects the oils beneath it in the new skin. We don't want you to worry. Now I'm just going to help you onto the gurney. Really, don't worry. You'll be sound asleep. The surgeon is like a geologist coming with a little saw to a geode. Inside the geode there are little crystalline teeth. At first they suggest the frozen grin on the faces of certain politicians when they have fallen asleep with their mouths open. Well, anyway, here we go. . . .

MORALITY PLAY

A curved path begins slipping away from the people on it. "I am sick of always being stepped on," mutters the path in its leaves as it leaves.

But the people, the people, their feet are left in the air!

To survive they become birds, and soon their droppings cover all paths, even Lao Tze's *The journey of a thousand miles begins with one step.*

There are always leaves muttering to themselves and birds unable to speak as people, and as usual the sky is over while the turds fall through.

Don't look for a moral; look for an egg or two.

THE PHILOSOPHER'S ASSISTED LIVING

In this up-to-the-minute hot-shot den of floating togas, ancient consciousness speaks in mid-air: I am Socrates, says one. His wife, Xanthippe, is also here, with their hovering sons who become obsequious and silently detached, like a logical outcome, and a fact.

Xanthippe tells her husband, Autumn's got its fingers through the trees again. Along the baring branches the owl feels exposed. No squirrel exchanges its fur with a mink. Under ground is a tight air-stream of voles with criminal pebbles blocking their way.

Are not the stones logical, asks Socrates? Please do not hurl that bucket of wash-water at me again, he pleads with Xanthippe.

All's well that fall's well, says Xanthippe. Floating in these togas we are like warm indoor clouds, husband, but your logic is a form of freezing, the icicles of thought are as daggers to the heart of intuition, so I am going out to find some early snow above voles, a flow of flakes above stones. Watch the kids, husband, and remember the ancients in our genes, while I become like the snow leopard among snowfields, my bespotted toga its colors, my heart beating the air to a pulse.

B.A.D.

The Becket Ambulance Department crew has been taking people with severe 'cabin fever' to the appropriate hospital, all right, those who are stir-crazy or worse. Those who are wild because feeling trapped in their houses on backroads in this hill-town in midwinter. 'Wind devils' of swirling snow in yards are downright spectral to them, so they booze or smoke into stupors, then wake to see the moon deepening its scars, bandages swirling around it, and howls in the stovepipe, enough to scare critters off a flea-holder. One woman, named Caresse, was found naked by her wood-stove. She had been seeing a black sun on the ceiling and had considered calling herself Clytoris, but settled on naming her whippet that instead. And when I ask the crew about any others they've transported they each tap their head with one finger to indicate the general craziness occurring among some people in town, and then they get down on all fours in the General Store and begin to bark. Someone should call for an ambulance.

YOLO

Things reducing to one, one thing. . .

any slug or dolt can read the outdated law still
"on the books" in Massachusetts: The Goatee
Ordinance, declaring it illegal to wear a goatee
unless one first pays a special license fee for the
privilege of wearing one in public. . .

and where the baby hobo slept, her two adults,
"bearded slugs of society," lay down beside her in
the ditch, and played dead. . . years since slugs,
trash, and upturned handlebars. . .

and to light the moment the casket was opened:
the shape and position of Salvador Dali's handle-
bar mustache, unchanged in the 28 years since
burial, "kept its classic 10-past-10 position" un-
der the museum's sluggishly melting watch. . .

and also 28 years later, in a garden bearded with
weeds, a living slug, physiologically a foot, com-
pleted its entry into, yes. . .

a long trek to get
here, under broccoli plants,
foot that drowns in beer.

READY FOR WORK

At different times throughout the day the lower half of a man's leg was dangling from the roof above my head. Sock looked clean, sneaker dirty. That's all I could see from my vantage point under an eave. Hammering went on all day, shingles thrown down, strips of metal, like metallic icicles, dangled and fell from the roof's edge, and there was drilling and rapid fire from a nail gun Even so, I fell asleep in the late afternoon.

I woke just before dusk. All noise from the roof had ceased. I pulled myself out of bed and dragged my way along the balcony under the eaves, then crawled down the steps. A ladder was still pitched against the roof. I was able to climb up, somehow, using only one leg and by hoisting myself with my arms. At the roof's edge I found the lower half of leg still there, and without anyone seeing, I stuck it back onto my stump. I would be ready for work the next morning.

BETSY

Combing her hands through her hair, Betsy felt the strands become the grain of a wooden coffin—she had always wanted to be buried in her hair.

Sad people bearing weird food and flowers appeared in her home and wept. She heard her friends read poems to each other.

She heard a high-pitched sound like a metal flagpole being struck forcefully by a sprinkler shooting rapid water. That's how she came to understand heaven's pitch, and that heaven's to Betsy as Betsy's to heaven.

She remembered certain lines from Byron:

The bright sun was extinguish'd, and the stars
Did wander darkling in the eternal space,
Rayless, and pathless, and the icy earth
Swung blind and blackening in the moonless air.

So Betsy climbed the stars. No visible fingerprints on the star-walls. Ugly-sister-hissy-fit comets hurled by in silence. She found black holes are a kind mosh pit full of Cinderellas waiting for the fit of a quantum slipper. No prince in the equation. There was, in the end, Nothing, and Nothing obtained to a first tendency, and that first tendency was to become woman. And the first sound was a high-pitched sound. . . sounding before anything else woke, sounding even before Naad and OM came to.

BLASCHKO'S LINES

Human bodies have stripes, scientists say, lines on our skin. The lines become visible under black or ultraviolet light, but they don't glow. Same pattern of stripes on all people, repeating down arms and legs, as if they are map lines for ancient destinations lost. How far back did the lines start, our first human ancestor, or before, passed over from some-thing other?

Where could they have led us, except to us? We travel our own bodies as blood courses its blue highways rising to the surface, raising on our invisibly striped limbs. The stripes must have hid us once from predators, as zebras are hidden in the tall African grasses because their lines blend with them against colorblind lions. Step out on the plains and you risk. We step.

There may yet be another type of light, one to reveal us and an early destination even before ancestors in caves. Or perhaps the lines trace old paths of starlight that once entered like veins inside our hearts. There may be a trace of what once first beat within every human womb, and which is occasionally picked up by a stethoscope, a lone doctor hearing the faint echo of a voice she cannot call human, and dares not tell anyone, not even at home. She wakes to wonder if anyone else ever hears that voice pulling night into higher space above the sun or cares that its sound comes from neither bird nor angel, but as bounced frequencies or a talent of lines from a star moving something, like a mouth of light.

KEYS

Miss Angina, or maybe it was Angelina, was my kindergarten teacher, more than 60 years ago. I've seen her many times throughout the years since I was five. "That's impossible," says my friend, "you've always told me she was very old back then." Well, okay, I guess I've seen so many hefty big-breasted white-haired women in my life so far, all looking more or less like Miss Angina. "Why do you remember her?" She was always bending over our desks and wore blouses with pretty low necklines, a bit strange for a classroom teacher, especially back then. A lot of times she would touch her chest. "So?" Well one day one of her big boobs popped out, jumped right out of her blouse, right in front of me at my desk. It seemed enormous. "Yeah, sure." No kidding, I didn't know what was happening, yet it seemed vaguely familiar to me. "Then what?" She quickly scooped up her pendulous pop-out and tucked it away again. "Yeah, sure, ha-ha." No, really. I remember her pointing to a scribble I drew of my mother on a piece of paper on my desk, while all the other kids in the classroom had photographs of their parents on their desks. "How come you only had a picture of your mother?" Well, I didn't really, because I had no mother, or no one I could remember. "Then what was Miss Angina pointing to?" My picture of a piano, one with big gleaming teeth. "Why would Miss Angina" point to it?" Probably because she couldn't tell its sex, whether or not it was my mother or father. All pianos are neuter until played, right? "I guess so." Ever since Miss Angina's breast dangled over the keyboard I have heard music coming from women's breasts. This isn't just a Romantic notion of pounding hearts, it goes all the way back to infancy and suckling and how mothers sometimes sing to their nursing infants. "If you say so. Didn't your father play piano?" He did, he could turn it into a woman. "Your mother?" She was long gone. I was still very small. I remember opening the lid of the keyboard and pretending that the keys were her smile; and once I filled a balloon with milk and placed it below, on the bench.

LEAVING HIS MARK

Today I found a dried black drop, a splotch on the hinged lid of my father's cherry desk, that part raised as a drafting table for him to write on onionskin paper with India ink mid-way in the 20th century, his long-stalked wooden pen dipping metal into an inkwell until the nib wrote music.

As a small child, I once watched from behind, until discovered, and was gently asked to leave this man who fancied himself in another century, with Chopin.

Later, in Carnegie Hall, all would hear what my father first heard out of the silence it took create his Modal Variations for piano, another master's hands playing it to applause.

That drop of black ink in cherry remains the note my father didn't write; I own it—a birthmark from silence.

BUONA NOTTE

Even now we are in the words we knew together,
and most in the Italian words we most used, and
I wanted to tell my father this when I saw him for
the last time before he died.

Now this sense of being poured, slowly, into
night, grains in an hourglass, but whose glass,
and is it really one? What really trickles between
chambers? Why do I sustain an appetite for loss,
for whom or what is missing in such silence as
sand spilling hours without numbers, without
voice?

My father's wristwatch
still ticking
in the casket.

NOTHING TO SAY, I SAY

She is dead-to-ashes, and we are gathered to
throw an orange rose into the Hudson, to satisfy
a final wish of this woman who bore and aban-
doned me, not yet four years old, and my brother
at six months, on a permanent

shore.

She was a daughter, sister and aunt, survivor of
guilt and suicide, who chose to cut

from her kids.

Now, with her niece, nephew, and her own
brother, I toss her favorite color into this long-
stemmed river, and walk back toward my own
sea—my brother on his own island, still

lost to me.

In Memoriam: Joanne Mathiasen

RESPONSE SIEVE

Poets, you know, are voyeurs-in-waiting, each wanting to peep through a pornhubble telescope: the star and verb naked, light and shade becoming adjectives dressing or undressing nouns, and so forth, she said he said.

That's also the way a painter may telescope vision to reveal pink or red in action or a blue mood nude, he said she said.

"All I ever wanted to do was to paint sunlight on the side of a house," quoting Edward Hopper, she said he said.

They are the same thing, for the eye may telescope and the sun shed on a house, they said.

Let's go off and discuss other conundrums under the sun, such as could snowflakes ever flub togethermelt or form a blend splendid as vanilla ice cream spilled splat on a black cloth, a mock Milky Way, or a white cow standing beside a black shed, its moo inside moon and mood, as you can hear, they thought they said.

CHALLENGE

I never painted dreams. I painted my own reality.
—Frida Kahlo

You're painting the room well, you think, rolling the ceiling, then rolling the walls, using brush where walls and ceiling touch.

You begin to feel the room gathering itself to receive what can't be covered: your shadow wanting to move beyond its darkness, desiring more than cast.

So now you know a challenge of poetry to embody home: walls and ceiling fresh as reams, and an alphabet of shadows becoming you, you think. You dream.

SPECULATION

As natural and initial as red ochre in Lascaux cave
paintings, considerations made then, thinking
toward others, mammoth and tiger and hunter,
became one view toward the origin of justice,
as in how to depict and balance the portions
and the threats.

RICKSHAW CHASM, 12 Graphs

For Joseph Hutchison

A Moment Before Waking

Best shadows are inside us. Never flood them with light! We all know about the worst shadows, such as the indecisive grays, all those that have come from harmful forces and influences from the world. Best shadows align us. It is all right to help them dance a little by shining a small light.

A Moment Before Breakfast

Reflected as in any metal spoon: your face up-side-down, placed into your mouth, withdrawn, blurred, wet-faced revenant of reflection, lampoon of spit, and wee pillages of torpor, all there is.

A Moment Before 9 a.m.

First frost has killed tomato plants overnight. Bent, glaucous, they will never stand again, they whose fruit was once blamed for occurrences of witches and werewolves; whose fruit were once called fruit and vegetable, until the political decision of the U.S. Supreme Court to deem them "vegetables". Don't osculate when you can kiss?

Indoors, I watch the last ones ripen on a platter next to a silver candelabra that with a few twists unscrews to become a single tall candlestick that with a few twists unscrews to stand as a squat one, resembling neither vegetable nor fruit, disassembled, yet standing as if in original silence waiting for light.

A Moment Before the Signpost

When the sign says Don't Go Past This Sky you know something's up. It might be a woman so pitched with her own internal night it stop-gaps the heart of a man trying to comprehend why the woman holds terrible dark stars and if she and they will exist in morning, a crescent moon still out like a fingernail's lunula, and what will sky say if she and the man wake and kiss without spunk and no lip-sync punk inner shadows stir?

A Moment Before the Voice Fades

After a drenching rain, I step out and hear the pond's usually mild waterfall three-tenths of a mile away rushing with the voice of an old woman screaming as she carries her childhood doll by its legs, the fall of its long hair across the spillway—In a lifetime, she yells, we come only once through such water with the water we are.

A Moment Before Imagined Obloquies

As the red squirrel drags an old brown rag splotched with dried engine oil and dropped outside our shed, why do I think of being a trained dog sniffing out the fecal in poetry?

A dandruff of snow begins on the rodent teeth-hauling its patch to nest, while I watch indoors and write to a friend of what stinks from latest printed appearances of MFA workshop clones flushed through the latest dung-let.

A Moment Before the Town Road Crew, Ratio: 5 To 1

While the men stand propped against their shovels and laughing as they watch the single woman on the crew dig hard-to-clear snow from town drains, they don't know she imagines all snowmen with their balls falling off and melting into the darkness below, until she tells them so.

A Moment Before the Pond Freezes

To watch snowflakes losing their marvels in the arctic deadpan, all the whorled a vanishing-trick.

A Moment Before Dusk and the Storm Inside You

Freshest eyes often belong to visitors; but it is that place itself creates the need for sight and more, not just the seeing, The poet's eye, in a fine frenzy rolling, but how place comes to be within you—

Have you ever met anybody who's really a-wake?

To keep to an honesty of what you don't know or sense yet of what you may see of those swift up-drafts of snow, for instance, crossing the lake in a fine frenzy squalling, in the need of place itself to be of blown flakes about to hit that fence—

And as imagination bodies forth
The forms of things unknown,

it is any storm inside you may come to know.

A Moment Before Turning To Another Channel

That fat viper, the President-Elect, center stage, is evil in full flood of light—therefore no shadow, only the slick floor; and we already hear, through loudspeakers, trumped-up ukases issuing from bleak nonsense suddenly becoming an upright being walking ahead into darkness, then slither-ing—White House Kremlin National People's Congress—snake, vodka, rickshaw chasm.

A Moment Before Desperation (Remembered)

No moment ever lashed itself to anything but itself; brash now is a going concern, as it was. For him it was like this: dice madly in the muck of luck, as in nicks of time, as in mock guardian angels—dots on cubes flying and rolling, then coming to, as in back from coma, as in coming awake to nourish with more than mere 'snake eyes.' That he never starved—came close to the 'lose' inside 'close.'

A Moment Before Sleep

Sleep has its pillar of night, weightless within the sleeper, its plinth with a small crack widening toward morning and dawning consciousness to spread horizontally; then you will be given an internal column of light to ingest until each night raises its pillar again and the gap at the base of your sleep shuts.

THE NEW OLD WAY

There is no actual room, but since I've given you two tiny stone doors, tablets really, and thrown away the keys, your choices are clear, Moe: either replace the locks, or accept the doors as lockless.

Either create a room for the doors, the tablets, or let them remain standing in the dirt and air of this mountain.

Inscribe the doors if you like, but think of that this way: like viewing iPad tablets with the same message from YHVH on Twitter: I AM THAT I AM.

Now believe, if you can, in what commandments I have issued, and while you simultaneously broadcast tweets through cyberspace, repeat to the air: *Thou shalt have no other fogs before me,* et cetera, on down to coveting.

Now hurl the doors (a.k.a. larger-than-life iPad tablets) into the crowd below this mountain.

Waddya expect, eh? I'm ~~tweaking~~ tweeting things a little. Some delusions deserve to be coveted.

THE CELLAR IN THE iPHONE

We were in a sort of progress, as if descending through open bulkhead doors, only the screens of our devices lighting the way. We had lost all solace and human touch, and conversation was grunts. Oh hell, we were as ghosts, phantoms that could never improve, even if they improvised. Soon, we fell into something like sleep.

Whether or not I awoke, I was alone. I saw a border collie herding ripe watermelons, plump as them, and for some reason I felt more than glum, with a deeper sadness I could not explain, despite the symbolic melon collie. I knew I must soon leave for something other than waking, other than sleep. There were rains from around the world falling everywhere around me, each drop in slow motion, somehow scratched, clawed rains with each droplet convoluted as if each were a tiny brain. I could feel myself vanishing into the earth with them. William Blake came to mind, "For a tear is an intellectual thing." I felt compelled and still intense enough to leave this note like a mote or drop in air:

(After I disappear

close the parenthesis

EXPLORATION: WHAT IS THE SMELL OF SPACE?

For John and Joan Digby (who can always use more space.)

What is the smell of space? Not your breath on snowflakes causing them to sublime—maybe a whiff of Lethe when time is fed its ripples.

Not Emily in Amherst scribbling poems on backs of shopping lists and chocolate-wrappers—maybe ions and lunar shifts in an open invisible safe.

What is the smell of space? Not a warehouse deathtrap filled with burning pianos—maybe Man Ray's brass tacks glued single-file to the sole-plate of a household iron.

Not the phooey of rocks made of mortar screwed to a climbing-wall—maybe loss of empathy, but we would lose sense and aromas of beauty.

What is the smell of space? Not water in our well, and not the water we mostly are—maybe scents of us coming through to each other as each other. Here—smell.

Not the lingering perfume of vanilla on your skin after a shower—maybe the original female sex organ, furnace of the reclining moon.*

What is the smell of space? Not any final waft of truth—maybe as astronaut Don Pettit claimed, after sniffing exteriors of helmets, suits, gloves, and tools after space-walks: *Sweet-smelling welding fumes. That is the smell of space.* To him. To us?

Not once—but once *again,* we give each other
space knowing infinity's the last of its kind.

*from *Alchemy of the Purple Coil* (anonymous, 12th century
treatise on sexuality. The female sexual organ is referred to
as the "furnace of the reclining moon")

FUGITIVE PHILOSOPHY, An Assay

Under harsh light and the questions we are trying
to come clear, as outlaws, they say, 'come clean' in
confession of crimes.

We are all under the same light, with harsh urg-
ings to reveal ourselves and what we know, even
those who have ruined their minds, native once
before wrong schooling.

But innately complex materials cannot be reduced
any more than original discoveries of what may
come clear only in being irreducible in complex-
ity.

The only crime, then, is no crime, but to be hu-
man, sometimes desiring to flee, but stuck under
the lights of what seems real, of what we find to
reveal, intricate as it may be.

ABANDONED TRAIN, A Letter

To Irene Willis

Yes, I do sometimes wonder how much more time we have until, disembodied, we might continue to live within the lines of poetry we wrote, in the sounds in the trains of thought and more; and I also wonder about the older everybody's constant refrain of where did the time go? As if there were one time, one sense of it, weary Tempus Fugit at it again.

But no matter how much, in poetry, we try say something as true now as it may be ahead, outside of time, so to speak, we may first become as abandoned trains, too rusted to move, sense busted in busted bodies, uncoupled from parts of ourselves, but maybe alert just enough to wonder what happened to the crew and if there are really passengers flying in and out of windows.

And what of the window panes, whatever they really are, in shards strewn inside and outside of us, sharp as an amorphous solid, like glass, in time returning to their compositional elements from conductorless stars?

Yes, I do sometimes wonder. . . .

ABOUT THE AUTHOR

DAVID GIANNINI's most recently published collections of poetry include *FACES SOMEWHERE WILD* (Dos Madres Press;) *SPAN OF THREAD* (Cervena Barva Press,) *AZ TWO* (Adastra Press,) a "Featured Book" in the 2009 Massachusetts Poetry Festival; and *RIM/WAVE* (Quale Press.) 14 of his chapbooks were published 2013-17 including *INVERSE MIRROR*, a collaboration with artist, Judith Koppel. His work appears in national and international literary magazines and anthologies. He was nominated for a Pushcart Prize in 2015. Awards include: Massachusetts Artists Fellowship Awards; The Osa and Lee Mays Award For Poetry; an award for prosepoetry from the University of Florida; and a 2009 Finalist Award from the Naugatuck Review. He has been a gravedigger; beekeeper; taught at Williams College, The University of Massachusetts, and Berkshire Community College, as well as preschoolers and high school students, among others. Giannini was the Lead Rehabilitation Counselor for Compass Center, which he co-founded as the first rehabilitation clubhouse for severely and chronically mentally ill adults in the northwest corner of Connecticut.

www.davidgiannini.com

OTHER BOOKS BY DAVID GIANNINI
PUBLISHED BY DOS MADRES PRESS

FACES SOMEWHERE WILD (2017)

FOR THE FULL DOS MADRES PRESS CATALOG:
www.dosmadres.com